Primeras damas/First Ladies
Michelle Obama

por/by Lucia Raatma

Editora consultora/Consulting Editor: Gail Saunders-Smith, PhD

Consultor/Consultant: Carl Sferrazza Anthony,
Historiador de la Biblioteca Nacional de Primeras Damas en Canton, Ohio/
Historian National First Ladies' Library in Canton, Ohio

CAPSTONE PRESS
a capstone imprint

Pebble Plus is published by Capstone Press,
151 Good Counsel Drive, P.O. Box 669, Mankato, Minnesota 56002.
www.capstonepub.com

Books published by Capstone Press are manufactured with paper
containing at least 10 percent post-consumer waste.

Library of Congress Cataloging-in-Publication Data
Raatma, Lucia.
  Michelle Obama / by Lucia Raatma.
     p. cm.—(Pebble Plus bilingüe. Primeras damas Pebble Plus bilingual. First ladies)
  Includes index.
  Summary: "Simple text and photographs describe the life of Michelle Obama—in both English and Spanish"—
Provided by publisher.
  ISBN 978-1-4296-6110-2 (library binding)
 1. Obama, Michelle, 1964– —Juvenile literature. 2. Presidents' spouses—United States—Biography—Juvenile
literature. 3. Legislators' spouses—United States—Biography—Juvenile literature. 4. African American women
lawyers—Illinois—Chicago—Biography—Juvenile literature. I. Title.
E909.O24R334 2011
973.932092—dc22   2010042267

Editorial Credits
Jennifer Besel, editor; Strictly Spanish, translation services; Ashlee Suker, designer; Danielle Ceminsky, bilingual book
     designer; Svetlana Zhurkin, media researcher; Laura Manthe, production specialist

Photo Credits
Alamy/Jason O. Watson, 16–17; Vespasian, 9
AP Images/Obama for America, 11; Ted S. Warren, 5
Corbis/Brooks Kraft, cover (right)
Getty Images/AFP/Mandel Ngan, 21; AFP/Tim Sloan, 19; Barry Brecheisen, 6–7; Mark Wilson, 1, 12–13
Landov/Chicago Tribune/MCT, 15
Shutterstock/Alaettin Yildirim, 5, 7, 9, 13, 15, 19 (caption plate); antoninaart, cover (left), 1, 10–11, 14–15, 22–23, 24
     (pattern); Gemenacom, 11, 15 (frame)

Note to Parents and Teachers

The Primeras damas/First Ladies series supports national history standards related to people
and culture. This book describes and illustrates the life of Michelle Obama in both English and
Spanish. The images support early readers in understanding the text. The repetition of words
and phrases helps early readers learn new words. This book also introduces early readers to
subject-specific vocabulary words, which are defined in the Glossary section. Early readers may
need assistance to read some words and to use the Table of Contents, Glossary, Read More,
Internet Sites, and Index sections of the book.

Printed in the United States of America in North Mankato, Minnesota.
092010   005933CGS11

Table of Contents

Tabla de Contenidos

Early Life

Michelle Obama is the first African-American first lady. She was born in Chicago, Illinois, on January 17, 1964. She grew up with her parents, Fraser and Marian Robinson, and her brother, Craig.

Los primeros años

Michelle Obama es la primera primera dama afroamericana. Ella nació en Chicago, Illinois, el 17 de enero de 1964. Ella creció con sus padres, Fraser y Marian Robinson, y su hermano, Craig.

born in Chicago, Illinois/nace en Chicago, Illinois

1964

Michelle and her mother in 2008/
Michelle y su madre en 2008

5

Michelle with Sasha (left) and Malia (right) in 2004/Michelle con Sasha (izquierda) y Malia (derecha) en 2004

15

First Lady

Barack was elected to the U.S. Senate in 2004. In 2007 he decided to run for president. Michelle helped with his campaign. She gave speeches all over the country.

Primera dama

Barack fue electo al Senado de EE.UU. en 2004. En 2007 él decidió postularse para presidente. Michelle ayudó con su campaña. Ella dio discursos por todo el país.

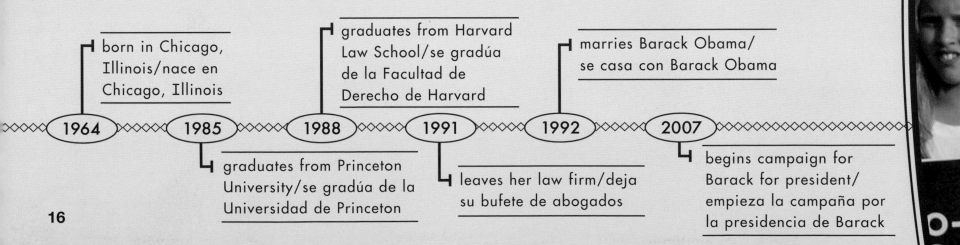

born in Chicago, Illinois/nace en Chicago, Illinois

graduates from Harvard Law School/se gradúa de la Facultad de Derecho de Harvard

marries Barack Obama/ se casa con Barack Obama

| 1964 | 1985 | 1988 | 1991 | 1992 | 2007 |

graduates from Princeton University/se gradúa de la Universidad de Princeton

leaves her law firm/deja su bufete de abogados

begins campaign for Barack for president/ empieza la campaña por la presidencia de Barack

WOMEN FOR OBAMA

WWW.BARACKOBAMA.COM

Obama

CHANGE
WE NEED

WWW.BARACKOBAMA.COM

In January 2009 Barack became president. Michelle became first lady. She grew vegetables at the White House. She wanted to remind people to eat healthy foods.

En enero de 2009 Barack se convirtió en presidente. Michelle se convirtió en primera dama. Ella cultivaba vegetales en la Casa Blanca. Ella quería recordarles a las personas que comieran alimentos saludables.

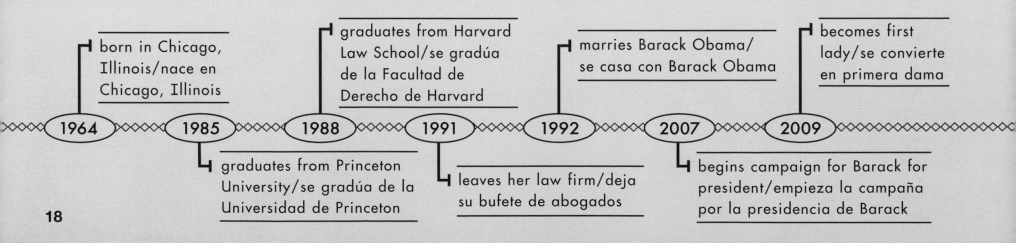

born in Chicago, Illinois/nace en Chicago, Illinois

graduates from Harvard Law School/se gradúa de la Facultad de Derecho de Harvard

marries Barack Obama/ se casa con Barack Obama

becomes first lady/se convierte en primera dama

1964   1985   1988   1991   1992   2007   2009

graduates from Princeton University/se gradúa de la Universidad de Princeton

leaves her law firm/deja su bufete de abogados

begins campaign for Barack for president/empieza la campaña por la presidencia de Barack

Michelle invited students to work in the White House garden./Michelle invitó a estudiantes a trabajar en el huerto de la Casa Blanca.

Carrot
Hercules

19

As first lady, Michelle travels the world. She talks
to people about volunteering in their communities.
She hopes to make the world better for everyone.

Como primera dama, Michelle viaja por todo
el mundo. Habla con las personas acerca del trabajo
voluntario en sus comunidades. Ella espera mejorar
el mundo para todos.

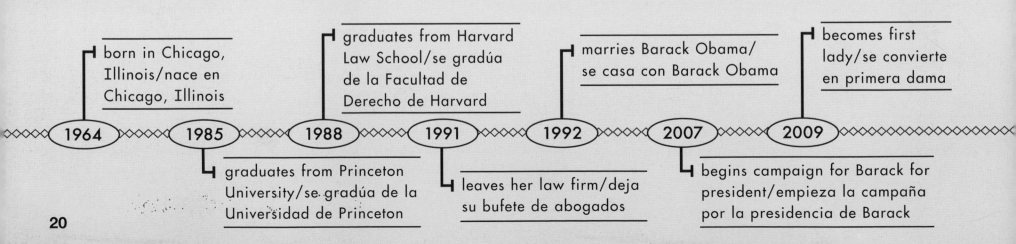

graduates from Harvard
Law School/se gradúa
de la Facultad de
Derecho de Harvard

becomes first
lady/se convierte
en primera dama

born in Chicago,
Illinois/nace en
Chicago, Illinois

marries Barack Obama/
se casa con Barack Obama

1964   1985   1988   1991   1992   2007   2009

graduates from Princeton
University/se gradúa de la
Universidad de Princeton

leaves her law firm/deja
su bufete de abogados

begins campaign for Barack for
president/empieza la campaña
por la presidencia de Barack

21

Glossary

campaign—an organized effort to win political office

community—a group of people who live in the same area or have something in common

elect—to choose a person for a job or task by voting

law firm—a business where lawyers work

Senate—one part of the Congress, which is a group of people who make laws

volunteer—to offer to do something without pay

Internet Sites

FactHound offers a safe, fun way to find Internet sites related to this book. All of the sites on FactHound have been researched by our staff.

Here's all you do:

Visit *www.facthound.com*

Type in this code: 9781429661102

 **Super-cool stuff!** Check out projects, games and lots more at **www.capstonekids.com**

Glosario

el bufete de abogados—un negocio donde trabajan abogados

la campaña—un esfuerzo organizado para ganar un puesto político

la comunidad—un grupo de personas que vive en la misma área o que tiene algo en común

elegir—seleccionar a una persona para un trabajo o tarea por medio de votos

el Senado—una parte del Congreso, que es un grupo de personas que hacen leyes

trabajar como voluntario—ofrecerse a hacer algo sin recibir pago

Sitios de Internet

FactHound brinda una forma segura y divertida de encontrar sitios de Internet relacionados con este libro. Todos los sitios en FactHound han sido investigados por nuestro personal.

Esto es todo lo que tienes que hacer:

Visita *www.facthound.com*

Ingresa este código: 9781429661102

¡Algo súper divertido! Hay proyectos, juegos y mucho más en www.capstonekids.com

Index

Índice